SHED ABROAD

Travel Edition

31-Day Devotional on God's Love

Dustin O. Martin

© 2017 Dustin O. Martin
All rights reserved.

ISBN: 1548452769
ISBN 13: 9781548452766

DEDICATION

With much appreciation I dedicate this book to the partners of Martin Ministries International. You have faithfully believed in our mission, vision and you have made your support to Mandy and myself visible through your love, prayers, and financial gifts. God placed this ministry in our hearts to support and build up the body of Christ, and He put the desire by the Holy Spirit in your hearts to assist us to accomplish this goal. **Thank you** for your love and your partnership in preaching the gospel of Jesus Christ.

DAY 1
"LOVES DEMAND FOR JUSTICE"

> **Isaiah 30:18 (AMP)** *And therefore the Lord [earnestly] waits [expecting, looking, and longing] to be gracious to you; and therefore He lifts Himself up, that He may have mercy on you and* **show loving-kindness to you**. *For the Lord is a God of justice. Blessed (happy, fortunate, to be envied) are all those who [earnestly] wait for Him, who expect and look and long for Him [for His victory, His favor, His love, His peace, His joy, and His matchless, unbroken companionship].*

We are all built with an inherent demand for justice. The reason for this is that we are all made in the likeness of our Father, God. When the twin towers fell on 9/11 we all, after our question of why was answered, wanted those responsible brought to justice for the wrong they had done. This cry for justice is a Godly attribute that strongly lives in the heart of every person.

The Father, being a God of justice, demands that any sin committed be made right and those responsible brought to justice. Instead of placing a bounty on the heads of the lawbreakers, God has made an eternal decision to give freedom to all mankind by paying the demand of justice by lifting up His only Son. This is love.

I want you to notice the desire of the Father's heart to satisfy the demand of justice was by lifting Himself up as a spectacle of shame, not for His own wrongdoing but because of His abundant love for us.

Love never demands what it is not willing to first accomplish and ensure for others. We love Him because He first loved us by sending Himself and satisfying justice's demand and ensuring His desire for all mankind would be made manifest and available. Because of this great demonstration there should be abundant exhibition of the fruit of love through us as joy, peace, patience, long-suffering, goodness, gentleness and self-control.

Blessed are those who "wait," or place their joyous expectation in God, seeking His response. The book of Hebrews tells us that those who come to God must believe that He is and that He is a rewarder of those who diligently seek Him. The love of God is displayed and ready to be revealed and expressed to those who expect Him. He is the supplier of all life's needs and requirements.

Because of this great act of love, we must require all that He is as a necessity to life and lay hold of it by faith.

Prayer: *Father, by the satisfying of justice through Jesus Christ, who was raised up for my justification, I receive today Your abundant supply of mercy and loving kindness. Amen*

DAY 2
"LOVE'S RESIDENCY"

1 John 4:16 *And we have known and believe the love that God has for us. God is love, and he who* ***abides in love*** *abides in God, and God in him.*

Love is not something that God merely possesses but that which describes His very character and person. As we become fully aware of the truth that lies within this verse, we will walk in the light that God has purposed for us from the beginning of time; we will live in Him and He in us.

The word *abide* here speaks of taking up residence and having constant habitation. Love Himself clearly gives us the definition and commitment of love's promise by declaring in Hebrews 13:5b, *"I will never leave you nor forsake you"* (emphasis mine). This statement of constant union is established through the work of Jesus Christ securing love's eternal occupancy and harmonizing the believer with the loving Father.

The importance of becoming aware of the love of the Father on the inside is one of the most important revelations a believer can be awakened to. For love will empower your faith, which supports your identity of authority and position as a child of the Most High God and silences the voice of fear; "because as He is, so are we in this world" (1 John 4:17).

To successfully abide in this revealed love of God, we must keep our spirits attuned to the desire and leadership of the Spirit and our minds steadily renewed to the Word of God. "Why?" you may ask. Because the Father's love never abandons us based on performance or lack thereof. When we allow fellowship with the Father to drift and our minds to conform to the world's way of thinking, we resist God's open arms and eternal love. We actually deny the Father's love, which has already been given to us. Through intimacy and the renewal of our minds, we begin to live in what is already, through Christ, living in us. This is where victory begins.

Prayer: *Father, I thank you that I am abiding in your love, and by Your Word and Spirit I am being renewed and strengthened daily. I choose today to reside in the love you have provided for me. I am living in Your love and Your love is living in me. I have complete victory over every situation I face, for I am loved by You. Amen*

DAY 3

"LOVE EDIFIES"

1 Corinthians 8:1b ...*Knowledge puffs up, but **love edifies**.*

This verse strikes a chord in my heart because building someone else up has always been one of my greatest joys. Those who know me know that I like to laugh and make others laugh if possible—yes, I was known as the class clown as a young man, for sure.

I remember once, when I was in first grade, our teacher had given all of us these very fragile, lightweight wooden airplanes that we put together and played with during P.E. Amid the ruckus of us throwing them, racing to go get them, picking them up and throwing them again, I saw one guy's airplane hit the floor just in time for another student to run by and accidentally step on it. I saw his face drop as he started to cry. I instantly ran over and placed my plane in his hands. He looked up, shocked and puzzled. "What are you doing?" he asked. I said, "Here you can have mine. I want you to have it." He was so excited he took off and started playing again.

There is such joy when a heart can be brought from despair to rejoicing all through an act of selflessness and kindness.

Natural knowledge and ability are self-edifying. Love forgets about itself and wants to hand its airplane to someone else, making sure to lift him or her up and build his or her image. Jesus, sent from God, is our airplane. Jesus' whole mission was to seek out and save people whose lives had been wrecked by sin. He was on a mission of love, to edify or build up the downtrodden. To take those who had been wrecked by sin, disease, lack and heartache, and place them back in the game of life with forgiveness, healing, supply and abundant joy. Luke 12:32 says, "Fear not, little flock; for it is your Father's good pleasure *to give you the kingdom*" (emphasis mine), and we know that the kingdom of God is "righteousness, peace and joy in the Holy Spirit" (Romans 14:17). Jesus came to replace your pain with His right standing with the Father—wholeness with nothing missing or broken and absolute joy in His Spirit.

Be encouraged. Love has come to reassure you of your success at His expense, so receive it and take flight, enjoying your day and knowing you have been made completely new and given all things that pertain to life and Godliness in the knowledge of Him (2 Peter 1:3).

Prayer: *Father, I receive today your gift to me of righteousness, peace and full joy. I will walk in the newness of life that has been provided and I will enjoy every moment being fully edified in and by your love. Amen.*

DAY 4
"LOVE'S MISUNDERSTOOD RESPONSE"

> **Mark 10:21** *Then Jesus, looking at him, **loved** him, and said to him, "One thing you lack: Go your way, sell whatever you have and give to the poor, and you will have treasure in heaven; and come, take up the cross, and follow Me."*

This is one of my favorite stories, for there is so much to see in the way Jesus responded to this young man; it's truly a peek into the heart of God.

Jesus was God's introduction of grace and truth to His people. This young man's training was not in grace, but in the Law of Moses. He revealed this when he asked the self-righteous question, "What must I do?" Jesus, loving him, wanted to shift the young ruler's perspective to God's love and way of salvation, which hinges not on earning but on receiving. The young man misunderstood Jesus' response, hearing only what was to be lost, and not what was to be gained. See, Jesus was working on the heart of this man. Although the riches of this young ruler had been an inheritance, his place with God had been earned through keeping the law. Jesus wanted him to see that his salvation was more like his inheritance—given. If the young ruler had understood this, he would have gladly taken the wisdom of Christ, knowing that salvation was not only his but also an abundant supply of wealth greater than his earthly inheritance.

Love has been misunderstood for too long. Read this closely: *Love is never trying to get from you, but always looking to give to you a supply for every area of your life.* This supply, when received, not only will enrich your life but will be so plentiful it also will supply for others' needs through you.

We must have a true understanding of Love's response and know that His invitation to follow Him is not an effort to strip us but instead to place the abundance of heaven in our hands to touch the lives of those around us with the gospel and all of heaven's resources.

Prayer: *Father, I receive Your supply of love for me today. I understand that Your love has given to me all that I may need in every area of my life, physically, emotionally, relationally and financially. Because I am so loved I will look for ways to allow this love to flow through me to those I encounter today. Amen.*

DAY 5
"THE KNOWLEDGE OF LOVE"

Ephesians 3:19 ... *to know the love of*
Christ, *which passes knowledge; that you may*
be filled with all the fullness of God.

The word *know* in this verse is understood as an intimate knowledge gained through a close relationship. If we are to continue growing in this knowledge of God, we must learn to cultivate a close fellowship with Him and stay sensitive to His leadings. When we do, we will execute the command of Christ by expressing this love to one another.

Living in this knowledge of love, which was received at the new birth and placed in the hearts of every believer by the Holy Spirit, we are then positioned to have Love's limitless depths revealed to us daily. Love's fullness satisfies the empty void in our hearts and causes a reaction that looks outward to express itself. We are not to be half-empty or even half-full people but people who overflow with God's presence and Spirit.

The idea seen here is that as we press into God, seeking Him, revelation will be released into our hearts, that we may, as it says in Ephesians 3:19 (Amplified Bible), "have the richest measure of the divine Presence that wholly fills and floods us with God Himself." The devil uses distractions of all kinds to chip away at the time we spend with the Father. If we allow this for any reason or make excuses, we don't lose the Father's love; we only forfeit the ability for Him to reveal the knowledge of His love in our lives.

Paul prayed this prayer because he longed for the church at Ephesus to grow in their walk with Christ and to continue to develop in the love of Christ. When love grows cold and stagnant, so will our faith. Yet when love is focused, the life of the believer will give way to the greatest victories.

Prayer: *Father, thank You for revealing Your love to me today. I will walk in the fullness of Your love and enjoy the richness of Your presence. I am not distracted or defeated, for I am loved. Amen.*

DAY 6
"ROOTED IN LOVE"

Ephesians 3:17 ...*that Christ may dwell in your hearts through faith; that you,* **being rooted and grounded in love...**

Working at a landscaping store in Tulsa, Oklahoma for four years, I learned the importance of planting properly. You don't just drop a tree in a hole and then pray it grows straight and strong. No, you make sure the soil is rich and well-nourished with nutrition, and then you saturate the hole with water, placing the burlap-covered root ball into the hole. It goes without saying that anything that does not stay planted will not grow successfully. A good friend said to me once, "Stick and stay—it's bound to pay." There's a lot of truth in that statement. Once you have planted your tree, daily watering will cause the roots to break through the stronghold of the burlap and stretch out for the substance in the soil.

For the revelation of Christ's love, which is shed abroad in our hearts, to flourish by faith, there must be a constant watering of the Word and praying in the Spirit. This daily watering of the Word encourages our faith, but faith without love is idle, for faith works by love (Galatians 5:6). Being rooted and grounded in love describes the picture of a believer who not only understands the requirement of living by faith but also is aware that without being planted continuously in love, true growth and abilities are cut short and left undeveloped.

Faith grows weak when it's not left to root and take nourishment in love. When recognized, love is the gateway to abundant joy and fullness of peace in our lives. If you allow the devil to discount and delude God's love, Satan will begin to restrict your spiritual stature and hinder your effectiveness in the lives of others.

We must stay rooted in love by keeping a steady gaze on Love's Word and guarding our hearts with all diligence; this way Love will root deep into the soil of our spirits and all that God is. By this our faith will continue to move mountains.

Prayer: *Father, I choose today to be rooted and grounded in love. I will not be uprooted by strife, unforgiveness or hatred for I forgive all wrongs and evil words spoken to me. I choose to stay planted in love, where my faith is energized and strengthened. Amen.*

DAY 7
"LOVE'S DEBT CANCELLATION PLAN"

Matthew 18:21-22 *Then Peter came to Him and said, "Lord, how often shall my brother sin against me, and I forgive him? Up to seven times?" Jesus said to him, "I do not say to you, up to seven times, **but up to seventy times seven…**"*

Jesus answers Peter's question about forgiveness, but His response is unexpected. The number seven in Hebrew language is the number of completion or perfection. When Peter says, "Forgive seven times," he would be justified according to the law, but according to grace, he is overlooking the truth. Jesus enlightens Peter with a number that leaves him and those listening puzzled, looking for an explanation. Jesus replies to Peter's statement saying, "I do not say to you, up to seven times, but seventy times seven."—or four hundred and ninety times— a day, every day, to every person. Jesus' point was that we truly love God's way not by keeping score but by forgetting the score and completely letting go.

Most read this parable and think, *"That's a good story and all, but I'll never let go of what so-and-so did or said to me."* Or, *"I'll forgive them but I'll never forget!"* This type of attitude is poisonous to the life of a believer. I understand letting go can be very challenging, but the one it holds captive isn't the offender—it's you. By focusing on the offense, you inflict a prison sentence on yourself. The offense becomes four walls surrounding you; unforgiveness becomes your cellmate. True freedom comes only when you decide to let go and let Love cancel the debt. The key to your freedom is found in the meditation of God's word and allowing Love Himself to remove the hurt and pain from your heart as well as the memory of its effect.

We must remember that God not only forgives us the debt of our sins but also places them into the depths of the sea (Matthew 7:19). If God forgave us our sins but never forgot them, how could He ever enjoy true fellowship with us? He would not be pleased with us; he would only be tolerating us, and no relationship will ever flourish in such an environment. The Word says that God has removed and forgotten our sins as far as the east is from the west (Psalms 103:12). His mind is filled with nothing but the desire to do us good and flood our lives with all His blessings.

Set yourself free today by letting go of all offenses and letting God be your avenger and justifier. You'll return to a life of joy and God will handle the delicate details, bringing you complete restoration.

Prayer: *Father, I choose today to forgive and forget the wrongs that have been done to me. I cannot control what others do and say to me, but I can control how I respond and what I allow to stay in my heart. I have received your love freely and will freely use that love to respond to others, staying full of joy and peace. Amen.*

DAY 8
"LOVE'S GREAT MYSTERY"

Ephesians 5:32 *This is a great mystery, but I speak **concerning Christ and the church.***

In writing to the church at Ephesus, Paul uses the covenant of marriage to bring clarity to the covenant of Christ and the church. He calls a man and woman becoming one flesh in marriage a great mystery, yet the true topic being revealed here is Christ and the church being made one together.

Reading the Word of God and hearing the preaching of the gospel of Jesus Christ are necessary to shed light on this great mystery; for it is in Him and by the Spirit of God that divine secrets and hidden truths are revealed.

There is an astonishing truth that must be known about the Father: He has chosen to love us as much as He does Jesus, making us one with Himself (John 17:23). His responsibility is the same as a husband to a wife: to love unconditionally in and through all trials.

He does this because, according to 1 Corinthians 6:17, "He who is joined to the Lord is one spirit with Him." This is Love's great mystery—I in you, you in Me.

He loves us because we are flesh of His flesh and bone of His bone. We do not hate our own flesh but nourish and cherish it, as does the Lord with His body, the church. God chose the marriage of a man and women to illustrate the covenant that He has made with us. Unfortunately, marriage has been attacked over the years by a twisted ideal that has tried to weaken and change its meaning. No matter what the world may say about marriage, God's decision to enter into a covenant of blood cannot be broken and is forever sealed. Jesus conquered death and was raised from the grave, sealing in our hearts the covenant of God's love. We are forever loved and made one with the Father.

We are one with Christ; as He is, so are we in this world. We are overcoming, holy, blessed, healed and made wealthy. We are filled with His fullness and will walk in it according to the degree we have rooted ourselves in Him.

Start today renewing your mind to what Love says about you instead of what the enemy has been trying to convince you of. Believe and walk in the oneness of the Spirit that you have in Christ Jesus.

Prayer: *Father, I know that I have been made one with you through Jesus and that you will never leave me or forsake me. You love me as much as you love Jesus. I am never alone to defend myself; You are always here to guide and protect me. Thank you, Father, for revealing this unconditional and steadfast love to me today. Amen.*

DAY 9
"LOVE'S PROPOSAL"

Hosea 2:19,20 (MSG) *And then I'll marry you for good—forever! I'll marry you true and proper,* **in love and tenderness***. Yes, I'll marry you and neither leave you nor let you go. You'll know me, God, for who I really am.*

The book of Hosea has always intrigued me. God had Hosea the prophet live out a real-life parable to illustrate the cheating heart of Israel and God's desire to take them back. God did this by having Hosea marry a harlot and then have children with her. After reading this story, I realized that the depth of God's love is truly unfathomable to mere men and goes beyond our natural understanding.

The Message Bible's introduction to this book reads, "*When our minds and imaginations are crippled with lies about love,* we have a hard time understanding this fundamental ingredient of daily living, 'love,' either as a noun or verb" (emphasis mine).

To start receiving the beginning depths of Love's proposal to us in Christ Jesus, we must first receive His forgiveness of our sins. Once we understand that Jesus has washed us from all wrongdoing, we can enter the life that is empowered by His grace and places us in abundant favor. Satan's job is to consistently cripple us with lies about the Father's love. Using the example of a parent or past relationship, he may say to you that there's no such thing as a love like that, trying to convince you that loved ones always end up leaving or hurting you. These lies rob us of the life the Father has purposed for us in Christ and hold us captive from living in complete satisfaction.

Remember God chose you when you were still His enemy and completely against Him in every word, action and deed. Yet, in Christ, He received you unto Himself as His own and loved you as if you had never sinned or committed wrong. I know—it blows my mind too. Yet this is what causes us to run to Him and long for His embrace every day. God is saying to you right now, despite yesterday's mess-ups and failures, "I choose you and I love you!" Every day when we wake up, we must decide that we will accept the Father's loving proposal, knowing we are completely and forever His.

Prayer: *Father, thank you for choosing me. I know that in Christ I am forgiven and taken as Your own. I will walk with the knowledge that my past has no bearing on my future, for Your only plans for me are good and full of hope. Amen.*

DAY 10
"LOVE'S CORRECTION"

Proverbs 3:12 *For **whom the Lord loves He corrects,** just as a father the son in whom he delights.*

Growing up in the Martin household, I was no stranger to correction. Being disobedient and talking back were just a couple of the door openers to a good old-fashioned spanking. Training children in the way they should go is no small matter; it holds the course of young people's future in its hands. When we become "born again" as children of God being made righteous in Christ, the question still stands: How does God correct His children to train them in the way of righteousness?

Religion has tried to answer this question with natural trials and afflictions, which cause people to run from God instead of to Him. God does not teach life lessons by handing out backhands.

We must remember that God is Spirit and reveals His love through His Word, which is Spirit and life (John 6:63). Because God is Spirit,

He trains and corrects us through and by the spirit. According to Mark 3:23–27, a house divided cannot stand. Meaning God does not will your healing and prosperity only to will it away in a time of correction; the kingdom of God could never stand this way. Natural trials are simply of the enemy, who deals in the physical, opposing the faith and stand you have decided to take where God's Word is concerned.

> **2 Timothy 3:16** All Scripture is given by inspiration of God, and is profitable for doctrine, for reproof, *for correction,* for instruction in righteousness.

> **John 14:26** But the Helper, the Holy Spirit, whom the Father will send in My name, He will *teach you* all things. (Emphasis mine.)

You see, God is love, and because He loves us, He teaches, corrects and instructs us through our recreated spirits in Christ. Love cannot and does not use pain, hurt, sickness or tragedy to bring about His will and promises. His will is determined in Christ and is made active as we believe and grow in our fellowship with Him. Our maturity does not come from hardships but from the feeding and leading of the Word and Spirit.

Prayer: *Father, because you love me, I receive your correction and instruction today. I choose to conform to your will and way by being quick to hear and slow to speak. As I learn to listen and obey, I will become a mature and responsible believer, fit for the Master's use. Amen*

DAY 11

"AWAKE LOVE"

Hebrews 10:24,25 *And let us consider one another in order to **stir up love** and good works....*

When vinegar and oil are mixed well together, they make a great salad dressing, but allowed to sit, and they will separate. If you give that bottle a vigorous shake, the two become one again, and you're back in business. Love, which has been shed abroad in our hearts by the Holy Spirit manifests through good works, which are the actions of a heart flooded with light, and are brought to life through the consideration of one another.

Nothing drains love and paralyzes good works better than critical judgment. The word *consider* here is the same word Jesus used in Matthew 7:3, "And why do you look at the speck in your brother's eye, but do not consider the plank in your own eye." In other words, love and doing good are awakened by the ability to forgive and walk with an understanding heart with those in our lives. Too many times we are quick to judge those we meet, not realizing that by so doing, we are stifling love and boxing up the good that God would have us do unto them.

When we consider one another, we are placing ourselves in their shoes. Consideration is produced by compassion, which can see the needs and hurts of others. **Consideration does not stop at what is noticed but looks to supply what is needed**, whether it's a simple hug, financial support or spiritual encouragement through prayer or spoken word. Jesus is the master of consideration. Sent by God to embrace humanity in all its self-inflicted and demonic suffering, He didn't consider Himself or His reputation but took the form of a bondservant, coming in the likeness of men. He became obedient to the point of death, and therefore God highly exalted Him and has given Him the name that is above every name (Philippians 2:6–9).

When we consider each other, we are awakening love and Godlike actions that produce results that reflect the heart of God.

Prayer: *Father, I ask you today to help me see others as you see them, as valuable and precious, so that I may love them and do good unto them as You have done unto me. I will not judge the actions of others but will, through compassion, look for a way to build them up and assist them in their walk with you. Amen.*

DAY 12

"LOVE'S HEART"

John 13:34-35 *A new commandment I give to you, that you love one another;* ***as I have loved you,*** *that you also love one another.* ³⁵ *By this all will know that you are My disciples, if you have love for one another.*

One of the greatest revelations that a believer can receive is that he or she can love another person only by and through the love of Christ. You will never be able to love your spouse or another person in your own strength or ability. John wrote in 1 John 4:10 that our ability to love comes directly from God the Father, who first loved us. Loving someone in and of yourself is impossible. The divorce rate, in both the church and the world at large, proves this. Jesus gave this commandment not to place us under a weight that none could carry, but to reveal how His grace would be used and manifested in our lives.

Ezekiel 36:26-27 says, "A new heart will I give you and a new spirit will I put within you, and I will take away the stony heart out of your flesh and give you a heart of flesh. And I will put my Spirit within you and cause you to walk in My statutes." Without Love's heart, without Love's Spirit in us, the command to love is unreasonable. Remember that when a command is given, the authority and the ability to carry it out are supplied. The Father can command us to love one another because He has placed the ability in us by His Spirit to do so. (Romans 5:5).

A natural, selfish or stony heart must undergo a transplant to truly love others the way God loves us. Without the indwelling of the Holy Spirit to take out the heart of stone and give us a new heart—Love's heart—we are miserable people forever lost in selfish works and desires. But when Love's Spirit floods our hearts with His character and nature, we become children of Love, empowered and enabled to love others with and by His love, revealing His character and person to the world. We become walking advertisements that show forth the heart of God.

Prayer: *Father, thank you for giving me Your heart. I will love others not in my own ability but through and by Your Spirit. I know that as I begin to conduct my life in this love, I will see victory in every area where the devil has tried to bring division and hardship. Your love has made me an overcomer in all things. Amen.*

DAY 13

"THROUGH HIM WHO LOVED US"

Romans 8:37 *Yet in all these things we are more than conquerors* **through Him who loved us.**

The phrase "*all* these things" covers more territory than you can imagine. No matter what battle we may be facing or mess we were left to clean up, it is covered by love. In Romans 8:36 Paul says, "Who shall separate us from the love of Christ?" and then proceeds with a long list of hardships. Notice that he doesn't ask "what" will separate us, but "who," which implies that whatever situation or hardship we may be facing is the handiwork of Satan, who is trying to get us to forfeit our rights and privileges as "more than conquerors."

Like Paul, we must become fully persuaded that the "Him who loved us" is greater than the "him who is trying to separate us" from love of God. There is no principality, power, or being that can remove God's love from us.

The love of God, although patient and kind, is not weak but full of power. It is this same force that raised Christ from the dead and has made you more than a conqueror. Next time the devil speaks of defeat, hurt, failure or lack, remind him that the same force that stripped him of his power 2,000 years ago lives in you and has raised you up and made you sit with Christ in heavenly places!

Love has all the strength you need to walk out of any problem. Remember, Love said in Hebrews 13;5, "For He Himself has said, "I will never leave you nor forsake you." And 2 Corinthians 2:14 says, "Now thanks be unto God who always leads us in triumph in Christ." The only way love has no effect in our lives is if we allow the carnal desires to pull us from the Father's will. Jude 19 – 21:

> 19. These are sensual persons, who cause divisions, **not having the Spirit**.
> 20. But you, beloved, building up yourselves on your most holy faith, **praying in the Holy Ghost.**
> 21. **Keep yourselves in the love of God**, looking for the mercy of our Lord Jesus Christ unto eternal life.

All these verses hold the key to consistent victory and will build you up in the love of God.

Prayer: *Father, I believe that, because of the love you have for me, I am more than a conqueror in all things. I always triumph in Christ and give no place to the devil in my life. I daily build myself up and guard myself in love by praying in the Holy Spirit and meditating in God's word. Amen.*

DAY 14
"TRUSTING LOVE"

Proverbs 3:5-6 *Trust in the Lord **with all your heart**, and lean not on your own understanding; in all your ways acknowledge Him, and He will direct your paths.*

The story of King David and Mephibosheth in 2 Samuel 9 is a great example of God's loving kindness toward mankind and man's need to trust the true intentions of the Father—namely that He intends to help us, not harm us.

I believe that God's hand of loving kindness is reaching out to us, faithfully and filled with promises that ensure a full and satisfying life. Oh, sure there are persecutions and hardships resisting God's plan, but as Paul stated in 2 Timothy 2:11, "Out of them all the Lord delivered me." All of God's promises for our lives are "yes" and "amen" and are to be counted on continuously.

You always trust *in* something—allowing all your weight to be held by it. Our trust must be in the knowledge of God's love, for it is the only force that can truly hold us without remembrance of past wrongs and yet declare truth concerning God's intentions. Those who dare believe, trusting in the Father's love, are lifted to a safe and secure position just like Mephibosheth. Ultimately, trust is what is exchanged for the promises or words of commitment that have been given.

Divine truth is a prerequisite to full trust, and complete trust is obtained when one believes that God exists and is a rewarder of those who diligently seek Him.

Without absolute truth, trust becomes fickle and easily transferred to other voices that promise abundance, security and fulfillment—yet their words are spoken with deception. Saul and his family had convinced Mephibosheth that David and his family had only harm and destruction awaiting him the next time their paths crossed, but the truth was David was longing to show his covenanted love to its sworn covenant partner.

Remember, what we place our trust in reveals what we believe to be true.

Prayer: *Father, I receive today your loving kindness in my life today. I believe that it will lift me up and place me in position to take hold of all the provision you have laid up for me through the covenant of love in Christ Jesus. I have been seated together with Christ in heavenly places. Amen.*

DAY 15

"ENTRANCE TO LOVE"

Psalms 5:7 (Amp) *But as for me, I will enter Your house through the abundance of **Your steadfast love and mercy**.*

The writer of the Amplified Bible injects the word *steadfast* right before *love* and *mercy* to emphasize the weight of the love God has for His people. This was a true revelation for King David, for this attribute of God was mostly heard of and never truly known in its complete light until Jesus manifested and revealed it in all its magnificent dimensions. This is the Hebrew word *hesed*, which is translated "loving-kindness" and is based on a blood covenant that is unbreakable.

As with King David, the door that we walk through as we approach God is the door of His abundant and steadfast loving-kindness. We know that the Old Testament Tabernacle was a building that had the outer and inner courts of the Holy of Holies, which was the place of the Ark of the Covenant and the presence of God. God had to be in a place separate from the people because they were not holy; they were sinners, in need of redemption and justification. God's presence lived in the tabernacle, but when Jesus became the ultimate sacrifice, redeeming mankind and being their justifier, God moved out of the tabernacle and into His people by the Holy Spirit.

When Jesus told His disciples in John 14:17 that the Spirit of truth would dwell with them and be in them, it puzzled them for they had known God only from a distance and as a mystery behind the great veil of the Holy of Holies. To think of God dwelling inside them was beyond their understanding of tradition and religious education. King David was truly prophesying of the door through which man and His maker would reunite: love.

> **2 Corinthians 6:16b**, "I will dwell in them and walk among them. I will be their God, and they shall be my people."

God moved into His new house and took up residence. We have become the dwelling place of the holiest God. It is God's love that destroyed the barriers that denied us access into the Holy of Holies and manifested presence of God. It is His love, exemplified in Jesus, that produces the freedom for us to come boldly to the throne of grace that we may obtain mercy and find grace to help in a time of need (Hebrews 4:16).

Prayer: *Father, I thank You that You live on the inside of me and that I can live in Your presence every day knowing that You love me completely. I am filled unto overflowing with Your person, which is Love. I will be aware of God inside as I go about my day, completely free from all fear and doubt. Amen.*

DAY 16

"LOVE'S SALVATION"

Zephaniah 3:17 (AMP) *The Lord your God is in the midst of you, a Mighty One, a Savior [Who saves]! He will rejoice over you with joy; He will rest [in silent satisfaction] and* **in His love** *He will be silent and make no mention [of past sins, or even recall them]; He will exult over you with singing.*

The only way God the Father can be in the midst of His people is by the effectual working of His love in our lives. This was brought to fruition in the complete work of Jesus on the cross of Calvary, the Mighty One and Savior, giving victory and liberation to all mankind from the oppression of the enemy. It is in His love that the memory of faults and wrongs dissipate.

The word *midst* here is defined as the inner part, the core of the man. Peter spoke of this inner man in 1 Peter 3:4: "Rather let it be the hidden person of the heart," and Paul said in Romans 7:22: "For I delight in the law of God after the inward man." These men were speaking of the recreated man on the inside, the man that had been enabled, through love, to experience the nature and life of God flowing in his spirit.

This verse in Zephaniah speaks of not only God's desire to be with His people but also the fact that He would accomplish the required works to satisfy His desire. The love of the Father was used to fulfill His purpose and reunite man back into His arms. The word *love* here in the Hebrew is defined as intimate love, a forming of a covenant, which tells of loyalty. Because we are joined through Jesus, there is nothing that can separate us from Him. The argument of separation from God's point of view has forever been done away with. God now sings and dances over His new love, the body of Christ, who is white as snow and absolutely precious in His sight.

Prayer: *Father, today I will rest in the love You have for me. I know that through Your love, and with silent satisfaction You will make no mention of any past wrongs. You dance and sing over me with joy. I am Your delight and the object of Your love. Amen.*

DAY 17

"LOVE'S PROTECTION"

1 John 5:18 *We know that **whoever is born of God** does not sin; but he who has been born of God keeps himself, and the wicked one does not touch him.*

This verse, when first read, implies that one who is born of God keeps—or, better translated, *guards*—himself, but let me remind you that in 1 John 4:8, we read that God is love. We know that God does not simply possess love as an object but that in Him abides and exists the characteristic of full and complete love. Let's now read 1 John 5:18 this way: "We know that whoever is born of Love does not sin; but he who has been born of Love is guarded by Him, and the wicked one does not touch him."

The love of God is a shield that surrounds you; the enemy cannot penetrate it. This is why the devil works so hard to keep you in a mindset of fear regarding yourself.

When we allow ourselves to become full of anxiety, it resists the protection of Love and enables the enemy to come and steal, kill and destroy. It's not that Love has let down His guard or dropped His end of the deal, but self-preservation resists the covenant help of Love and says, "I got this," when in reality we need all of Love's strength, power and protection that has been given. Love bears up under anything and everything that comes and will take the weight of your situation (1 Corinthians 13:7). Love, through righteousness, goes before you, making ready all things, and its glory is your rear guard (Isaiah 58:8). Living in Love and allowing Love to be your safeguard in health, finances and relationships is the safest and most protected way you can live your life.

Next time the devil tries to attack—and trying is all he can do—stop and speak these words: "I am born of Love and Love guards me, therefore, Satan, I resist you and render you harmless and ineffective in my life in Jesus' name. I am safeguarded against lack, sickness and stress through the love of Christ!" Remember when Jesus was raised from the dead He became the enforcer of the covenant of love that the Father has made with you and me.

Prayer: *Father, I will live in the protection of Your love. I will not allow anxiety and worry to instill in me fear for what the future may hold. I know that You love me and have given Yourself for me. I will live in the secret place of the Most High and under the shadow of His protection. Amen.*

DAY 18

"LOVE IS HERE TO STAY"

Isaiah 54:10 (AMP) *For though the mountains should depart and the hills be shaken or removed, yet **My love** and kindness shall not depart from you, nor shall My covenant of peace and completeness be removed, says the Lord, Who has compassion on you.*

This verse is loaded with revelation; I can't help but get excited every time I read it. I have previously mentioned the Hebrew word *hesed*, which translates to love and kindness.

Hesed is equal to the Greek word *agape* and is defined as God's faithful love in action, which is faithfully persistent and unconditional in its outlook of man. It's tender, kind and merciful, and is God's relational mindset, which seeks out mankind, showing Himself as the lifter of their heads and remover of all their shame. It's a term used when cutting a blood covenant broken only through death. Through His death on the cross, Jesus broke the covenant of death that Satan had with man, and because Christ lives forever as our intercessor of the new covenant, it will never be broken or annulled.

I love the statement in this verse that God's loving-kindness is eternal. Natural things may come and go, but **God's love for you is here to stay.** Loving you is a decision based on God's will, determined and accomplished through Jesus Christ. As we live in Him, we have a sure foundation that will never crack, shift or fail. A life that is found in such a relationship is bound for greatness as God takes the reigns and steers us toward His unlimited source of care and provision.

What I want you to meditate on is this: everything may change and pass away, but God's *hesed* for me is forever; it is perpetual and ready to assist me every day and in every moment.

Prayer: *Father, I choose today to live in your peace and perfected love. I refuse to look at the changing factors of my life and I will not allow them to steal my joy, for I know that you are faithful and You are constantly watching over me. You are the lifter of my head and remover of all shame. Amen.*

DAY 19

"LOVE AND FAITH"

Galatians 5:6b ...*but faith working through love.*

This scripture provides some of the most important information concerning the forces of love and faith. Faith holds a huge part in the life of a believer; it's the hand that grabs the unseen, making it a reality, yet faith lies paralyzed without love. Why?

The answer to this question is found in the beginning of our opening verse, Galatians 5:6a, which reads, "For in *Christ Jesus* neither circumcision nor uncircumcision avails anything" (emphasis mine). In other words, our own actions to stand right before God give no strength to our faith. It is by grace that you are saved through faith.

When one receives Jesus as Lord and savior, the work of fulfilling the law is accomplished in Him. Jesus said in Matthew 5:17, "Do not think that I came to destroy the Law or the Prophets. I did not come to destroy but *to fulfill*" (emphasis mine). Paul wrote in Romans 13:10, "Love does no harm to a neighbor; therefore, love is the fulfillment of the law." Faith climbs to its highest ability and produces its greatest results when it's backed by love's accomplished work of satisfying the demand of justice. Faith will always come short of its desired goal when it's launched from self-effort. Faith is never found stranded on the side of the road of life when love is in its tank.

NOTE: Faith works by love but faith without corresponding action is dead. Not saved by works, but saved for good works. Love will fuel your faith while action solidifies it.

Prayer: *Father, through Your love, my faith is made alive. My faith rests in the work of Jesus Christ, who is Your commissioned love. I live by Jesus' fulfillment of the law, and therefore I am pleasing in Your sight. Your will is manifested in my life by my faith that is made active by corresponding actions of love. Amen.*

DAY 20

"LOVE'S WORD"

John 1:1 *In the beginning was the Word and **the Word was with Love** and **the Word was Love.***

1 John 4:8 established that God is Love. I would encourage you to practice replacing the name *God* with the word *Love* to assist your mind in seeing and receiving all that Love holds and His place in your life as a believer. To practice this, read 1 Corinthians 13:4–8 in the Amplified Bible, and where you read the word *love*, replace it with *God*. Then because you are born of Love (1 John 4:7), insert your name; for as He is, so are you in this world.

The word of Love plays a major role in our relationship with the Father and how we appropriate His promises in our lives. Hebrews 10:17 tells us that "faith comes by hearing and hearing by the Word of Love." If we don't have a correct understanding of who Love is, then when Love speaks to us, our faith is devoid of its ability and life-altering power. Faith operates by love, and with no understanding of love, faith cannot move or change the situation in your life (Galatians 5:6).

A person is only as good as their word. We all have room to grow in this area, but Love's Word is consistent and full of righteousness. It's not just the integrity of God's word that we must believe but also the unfailing faithfulness of the One who is speaking the words to begin with. The thoughts we entertain about Love are the most important things about us. If we have low and abased thoughts, then our expectations of Love will be shallow and full of uncertainty. Yet if our thoughts soar on the revealed knowledge of Love Himself, then our faith in His word will never leave us barren of fulfillment.

Love and His word are one, and to know Love, you must know Love's word and become rooted and grounded in it. This produces the faith that is undaunted by fear, doubt, failure and criticism. What makes most give up will only cause you to rise, breaking into praise as you have been delivered from the power of darkness and conveyed into the kingdom of Love's dear Son, Who is full of power, kindness and security.

Prayer: *Father, You are love, and as you reveal yourself through your Word, I will live in its light. I know that if You said it, You will bring it to pass; if You spoke it, You will make it good. I am convinced through your love for me in Christ Jesus that Your word is to be trusted and completely relied on. I will trust Love's word today. Amen.*

DAYS 21

"TRUE LOVE"

1 John 3:16 *"By this **we know love**, because He laid down His life for us."*

True love must be defined and demonstrated by its author. As we have studied previously, God defines true love, for God is love. For us to know love, there had to be a sacrifice of the will and self, which Jesus humbly and obediently accomplished. This world, with its mission to satisfy its own will and lusts, is passing away (1 John 2:17).

When God demonstrated His love toward mankind, it was while we were still ruled by all that opposed His will. Jesus died not to provide a tolerance of sin and death but, by grace and through faith, to give life to those bound by sin and subject to death. This is the true definition of love. The world believes that love is something that accepts and approves of the decisions of man and places this self-centered will as the power that conquers all. The only problem with this definition is that it leaves man alienated from God and still dominated by death. True love does not tolerate the self-destructive nature of sin but makes a way for escape so that true life can be obtained and lived in its entirety. Love does not work with the old nature but instead creates a brand-new nature that has God, Love Himself, in it to both will and do for His good pleasure.

We cannot mix the truth of God with a lie and expect positive results. The fruit of God's love, goodness, forbearance and patience leads us to turn from self-indulgence toward the love of God, which does not condemn but, through love, saves to the utmost.

It all comes down to first knowing God, believing that He is and that He rewards those who diligently seek Him (Hebrews 11:6).

Prayer: *Father, I know You love me because You have given Yourself for me. I will live in this purchased and given love of Jesus Christ. I will not seek to define love as the world does but, by Your word and spirit, accept the love You have given for me and allow it to be the deciding force in my life. Amen*

DAY 22

"UNLIMITED LOVE"

1 Corinthians 14:33 *For God (love) is not the author of confusion, but of peace....*

I was thinking of areas in life that have enforced limits, such as credit cards and highways. How fun would it be to spend without limit, with no responsibility to pay? Think about it—driving your car or motorcycle to its created potential without any threat of crashing or getting a ticket? Both limits are given for the protection of *self*. Why? Because where "self" is a priority in one's life, there will always be recession and ruin.

Galatians tells us that someone living by his recreated spirit produces love, joy, peace, patience, kindness, goodness, faithfulness, gentleness and *self-control*; against such, there is *no law*. No law, because love has cleared the debt and released the throttle of power that nullifies the effect of the law. Restriction and limit were created to prevent self-ruin. Limits control chaos, but in God, in Love, there is no confusion or disorder, for Love sets out to provide, protect and promote the well-being of everybody, forgetting about self-preservation.

We are born of God, birthed by Love, and as we step into this new nature, by grace and through faith, we will live in the position that is given liberally and supplied adequately by the Spirit of God in all its fullness and perfection. As we meditate and renew our minds to the truth of God's love and abandon self, we will know no bounds. We will step into the place of no limits and abundance in all things.

From the beginning, Jesus was about His Father's business. Jesus was never about Himself, for he was not seeking His own will, but the will of the Father who sent Him. This is the key to no limit. God's love in us will never insist on its own rights or its own way, for it is not self-seeking (1 Corinthians 13:5). It never does according to its own will. The freedom that is ushered in by the releasing of being "self-aware" and its care is refreshing and revitalizing. We become fatigued finding our own natural limits and resources when we focus on taking care of ourselves as our main daily duty. We are called to live in Him, and as we do, we will see the natural barriers removed.

Prayer: *Father, I will live in Your unlimited resource of love. I will seek not my own will but the will of the Father, who loved me and gave Himself for me. This is a life of more than enough, with ample supply in every area. Amen.*

DAY 23
"LOVE'S TRUE CALCULATION"

1 Corinthians 13:5b…Love (**God's love in us**); takes no *account* of the evil done to it [it pays no ATTENTION to a suffered wrong].

As we saw in Romans 5:5, God's love has been placed in our hearts by the Holy Spirit. The only thing that God is keeping tabs on is seen in Malachi 3:16:

> Then those who feared the Lord talked often one to another; and the Lord listened and heard it, and a book of *remembrance* was written before Him of those who reverenced and worshipfully feared the Lord and who thought on His name. (Emphasis mine.)

Love is not counting wrongs or past failures. His only thoughts toward you are, as Jeremiah 29:11 describes, "thoughts of peace and not of evil, to give you a future and a hope."

The power of this ability to "take no account and pay no attention" of others' wrongs is set in motion when we understand and accept the work of Jesus Christ in our own lives. Truly accepting and believing that, through Jesus, God has completely forgiven us and set us free from the debt of sin. Remember that, in yourself, it is impossible to love anyone the way God loved you, especially those who seem unlovable; however, when you, through the revelation of Jesus, understand what has been deposited in you by the Holy Spirit and your own forgiveness becomes clear, you then allow that love in you to love others through you. Then also, you begin to see God do what only He does—the impossible.

We read in 1 John 4:9, "In this was manifested the love of God toward us, because that God sent his only begotten Son into the world, that *we might live through him*" (emphasis mine). Living through Him is living in and by the law of love toward others, knowing that God is not holding our transgressions against us but has wiped out the written requirements against us, nailing them to the cross of Christ (Colossians 2:14). We too ought to practice the art of **losing count** where others are concerned and begin to love them with the love of Christ.

Prayer: *Father, just as You take no account or keep record of wrongs I have done, I choose to forget the wrongs that others have done toward me. No matter what is said or done today, I will respond in love and take no account of it in my heart. I forgive all. Amen.*

DAY 24

"LOVE VS PRIDE"

1 Corinthians 13:5 (AMP) ...*Love is not conceited (arrogant and inflated with pride); it is not rude (unmannerly) and does not act unbecomingly.*

Don't allow the repetition of this next phrase to stop you from hearing its truth: God is love, and the Holy Spirit has placed Love's ability in our hearts. This love enables us, when we submit to it, to respond correctly and overcome any situation with joy—God's true strength.

Know this: the number one weapon the devil has against believers is short circuiting the power of that love in their hearts by getting them to focus on self rather than depending on love's given grace. When we become self-aware, two things happen: a) we begin to believe that we are sufficient in ourselves, and b) we become overwhelmed and overcome by the weight of lack in all things.

Both are danger zones that paralyze Love's ability in us and put us out of the reach of Love's effect, not by His choice but our own.

James 4:6 says, "But He gives more grace. Therefore, He says: God resists the proud, but gives grace to the humble."

Pride is the opposing force of love. Like two magnets, they naturally oppose each other. When you are self-aware, instead of protected by love, your responses will be rude and disrespectful, reflecting your concern with your rights and protection. When God had the right to respond to us in a condescending way, He chose instead from the greatness of His character to respond by sending Jesus, who is love in action, to raise us up to His standard and level. We are seated with Christ in heavenly places far above all principality and power and might and dominion (Ephesians 1:20–21; 2:1–6).

Love doesn't respond harshly because love is not concerned with its own interests or person; it has one concern, and that is the well-being of others. Love asks, "How may I serve you?" Love is consumed with thoughts toward the needs of others and the way to supply those needs. When this truth resonates in our hearts with the power that it holds, we will step over into the understanding of God's place and response to our lives, and how we are then in turn to respond to those around us.

Prayer: *Father, I cast all my care of family, career and self over on You. I know that You care for me and that my pride pushes you away from areas where I need you most. I therefore humble myself under Your mighty hand and know that You will exalt me, having placed me in a place of abundance and favorable prominence. Amen.*

DAY 25

"LOVE, SUFFERS LONG"

1 Corinthians 13:4 (NKJV) *Love suffers long and is kind....*

When we read the term *suffers long*, our minds tend to drift to the idea of one who is going through a hard time, one who can take a continuous beating, tolerating the never-ending and countless blows of the enemy. Allow me to adjust your perspective on this term.

To suffer long is not to tolerate the beating but rather not to lose heart; patiently and without offense overcome the attack through the authority of Jesus. Have you ever noticed how some never seem to get out of the fiery battle? Religion has too many believing that God is trying to teach them something, and therefore they allow the enemy to continually bring hardship into their lives. This is not the meaning of suffering long. When love gets a hold of you, you will go through the fire, but you will quickly quench every flame to emerge completely victorious, not even smelling of smoke, for love Himself is with you and is guarding you.

This is why love is the foundation of our belief.

Notice the passage from Hebrews 12:2: "Who for the joy that was set before Him, endured the cross." Although the word *endured* here is not the same Greek word used in 1 Corinthians 13:4, it holds the same meaning and thought, which is to remain in strength and patiently receive the promise. Joy is the result or fruit of love active in our lives. Nehemiah 8:10 reminds us that the joy of the Lord is our strength. Therefore, love known and active in one's life will produce the strength and ability to come out of any fight victorious.

Love will have you saying words such as Paul said in 2 Corinthians 4:8-9: "*We are* hard-pressed on every side, yet not crushed; *we are* perplexed, but not in despair: 9 persecuted, but not forsaken; struck down, but not destroyed." Love is the ability to suffer long, to hold ground with patience. It's the love of God that has been given to make sure that you will never fail. It enables you to look at the trial and keep both hands lifted in thanksgiving, as you know victory is already yours.

Prayer: *Father, I give You thanks and praise in advance for the victory I have over the enemy's ploys and efforts to attack me. In the joy of the Lord, I will stand strong and full of courage, knowing the dawn of a new day is here and I am fully equipped for it in Christ. Amen.*

DAY 26

"LOVE'S RESPONSE"

Proverbs 24:17 (AMP) *Rejoice not when your enemy falls, and **let not your heart be glad when he stumbles** or is overthrown....*

Golf is typically known as a gentlemen's sport because of the considerate nature of the game. Stepping over the path of your opponent's putt, and standing quietly while he drives the ball down the fairway are just a couple of the courteous ways one shows respect to his fellow golfer. As we know, not all sports are created equal as some paint a different image when it comes to sportsmanlike conduct. Pushing, yelling, taunting and belittling are just a few of the actions of some when others miss the shot or make an error on the field.

When Adam and Eve lost against Satan and fell in the garden, God did not stand back and laugh at them, saying, "You fell for that lie? You idiot!" No, God took an animal and killed it, shedding its blood to atone for their sin and cover their once-glorified bodies with the fur of an animal. God's response to man's fall was not a celebration to shame them but a response of care and supernatural support. God did what He could in the moment by atoning for their sin with blood, and then He began to declare the coming Messiah, Who would bring man back to his rightful position as a child of God.

Love doesn't spike the football and taunt the exposed wrong and failure of others but looks for a way to lift up and protect the vulnerability of the wrecked individual. Proverbs 10:12 (AMP): "Hatred stirs up contentions, but love covers all transgressions."

Seek ways to allow the love in you to respond to those who have fallen or missed it around you. Find ways to assist them by bringing them back to fullness instead of finishing them off as they lay wounded.

Prayer: *Father, thank you for giving me a heart of compassion and the ability to see those who have done me wrong or have sinned willfully against me as valuable and precious. By faith I receive wisdom to see past the hurt to what may be the underlying issue that they are facing. May I be your hands and voice that positions them back to a place of healing and wellbeing. Amen.*

DAY 27
"LOVE'S FOUNDATION"

> **Ephesians 3:17** (AMP) *May Christ through your faith [actually] dwell (settle down, abide, make His permanent home) in your hearts! May you be rooted deep in love and **founded securely** on love....*

When we accepted Christ as our Lord and Savior, a foundation of love was placed in our hearts, for Jesus is the sent and displayed love of God. However, if this foundation is neglected and not taught, one's faith will begin to crack and shift, falling short of the promised potential.

The knowledge of God's love must be a priority in our lives. Love is not just the expressing of emotion; it's the institution of our success. 1 Corinthians 13 clearly states that the forces that fortify the heart of a recreated believer are all for nothing without love. All spiritual gifts, faith, community outreach, great sacrificial giving and becoming a martyr are fruitless without it. Yet this expression of love will never operate in its richness until we come entirely and intimately to know Christ's love for us. To grow in the love of God, we must daily water the foundation with His word, firmly planting and grounding ourselves in it, receiving revelation of its exhibition.

Loving others must come from the perfected and matured love that abides in us. See, I believe that when we are made aware of how much God abundantly loves us, we will understand the level that He desires us to operate from. Romans 8:32 says, "He who did not spare His own Son, but delivered Him up for us all, how shall He not with Him also freely give us all things?" God's love was without restraint or regret when He paid the extravagant price for our salvation through His Son, Jesus Christ. There was no turning back for Him; we were His prize and ultimate desire. After accomplishing this, the Father placed this same limitless love in our hearts, so we would pursue and love Him with the same resolve.

This amazing love affair between God and His man is the foundation that catapults us into a realm of success and ability. We must awaken to this amazing love and, by our energized faith, take hold of its vigor and capacity in our lives. As we do, visions will be accomplished, lives saved, bodies healed and needs abundantly met.

Prayer: *Father, thank you for laying the foundation of love in my heart that I may build a life of success. As I meditate on Your love for me, I will walk in the realm that You desire for me in Christ, being fully supplied and able to assist others with Your love. Amen.*

DAY 28
"THE KNOWLEDGE OF LOVE"

> **Ephesians 1:17** (AMP) *[For I always pray to] the God of our Lord Jesus Christ, the Father of glory, that He may grant you a spirit of wisdom and revelation [of insight into mysteries and secrets]* **in the [deep and intimate] knowledge of Him.**...

After Moses passed away, the position as the leader of the children of Israel was divinely given to Joshua. God gave precise instructions to Joshua on his new office by informing him what to think, see and say. Joshua 1:8 says,

> This Book of the Law shall not depart from your mouth, but you shall meditate in it day and night, that you may observe to do according to all that is written in it. For then you will make your way prosperous, and then you will have good success.

The instructions really were simple—God wanted Joshua's number one pursuit and focus to be Him, not leading or conquering.

Being able to lead and bring the children of Israel into a promised land of rest was not only secondary but would be impossible without the knowledge of God and understanding of His nature, character and way.

If we are to accomplish our missions, we, like Joshua, must know God. And for us to know God intimately, there must be a revelation of His love. Jesus is the manifested love of God in all its extravagant dimensions. I believe that as we come to confidently know and unwaveringly believe in the love God has for us, we will operate boldly and live fearlessly. I believe that doubt cannot coexist with absolute knowledge; God revealed is doubt removed.

Prayer: *Father, I thank You for giving me eyes that see and a heart that understands the love You have for me. I believe that as I grow in this knowledge of Your love I will accomplish the call You have placed on my life. I will make Your love my first priority by placing Your word before me daily and speaking it over every area of my life. Amen.*

DAY 29
"LOVE TURNS FEAR OUT"

1 John 4:18 *There is no fear in love; but **perfect love** **casts out fear**, because fear involves torment. But he who fears has not been made perfect in love.*

Too many have never taken the steps that God has placed in their hearts because failure feels surer than the success the Father has destined them to live. God's love is the only antidote for that fear of failure, which stifles the success we know we are called to achieve.

Love is more than the emotion of affection. The love of God is the choosing and deciding factor in all He does. It's a force that knows no boundaries and yet chooses to empower the lesser by its abilities; therefore, our success level is found in the knowledge of His love. To pursue love is to pursue the God of love and to intimately know the power that lies within its salvation. It's the simple idea of knowing not only the Word of God but the God of the Word.

We will never operate on the level that we should until we begin the journey of allowing the Spirit of God to expose and reveal the greatness of that which has been placed in our hearts by His love. Building on this love and operating from it are the steps that carry us to greater things as fear is completely evicted from our hearts.

When we place ourselves completely in the truth of God's Word, we will begin to live as He desires us to. There may be opposition to the Word, but never absolute defeat, for His love ensures His absolute care and overflowing fullness, which is found in Christ.

We are to pursue love because it's the ingredient that empowers us to live at the level that God desires. The love of Christ is the model we are to receive and follow as we are filled with the fullness of God. The love of Christ was perfectly personified in Jesus' daily walk as a man, never knowing lack, sickness or worry. Jesus dominated the forces of the enemy by the love of God, as it removed all fear. He continually encouraged those who walked with Him or came seeking Him to live above it by having faith in God.

This is why love employs our faith in obtaining levels of greatness that the natural mind has never dared imagine. May the Father's love destroy all fear in your life as you step out in faith and live in full satisfaction.

Prayer: *Father, I am free from all fears and choose to live in Your love, which never fails. My life is found in Christ and I will operate by the love of the Spirit. I cannot fail, for I am more than a conqueror in Him who loved me and gave Himself for me. In the life that I now live, I live by faith in the Son of God. I am always victorious in all things. Amen.*

DAY 30

"LOVE'S ASSIST THROUGH PRAYER"

> **John 16:7** *Nevertheless I tell you the truth. It is to your advantage that I go away; for if I do not go away, the Helper will not come to you; but If I depart*, **I will send Him to you.**

Have you ever been working on a project and found yourself with a drill or hammer in one hand and a curtain rod or shelf in the other, all the while balancing on a ladder? If so, you may have thought, *I could use a little help here!* Or, *Can I get a second hand please?* I know this is a common occurrence for me when I'm trying to hang or build anything, as it's not my expertise. I also know that God always places nearby friends who are quick to respond.

Thank God we are no longer waiting on help. God sent the Helper two thousand years ago as He broke the envelope of the atmosphere in Jerusalem in the upper room. The Holy Spirit came to each of those 120 folks and filled them with much-needed help for their assignment at hand.

This help that God has so graciously provided is brought to the forefront of our lives when we turn from complaining and wondering about how it will all work and begin to pray. I want to encourage you in your prayer life to fan the flame of intimacy with the Father. Prayer is a mighty tool that God has placed in our arsenal against the enemy. It's mighty because we are not praying alone about the needed help but in complete oneness with the Father and the Holy Spirit, meaning we can accomplish great feats.

You see, it's in times of prayer that we position ourselves to hear the voice of the Good Shepherd. It's where our help comes from; it's the source of our directions. Romans 8:26 says, "Likewise the Spirit also helps [takes hold together with us against] in our weaknesses." When we sit at the feet of Jesus, we will be given all things that pertain to life and living in His divine character of love.

This communion is the language of love, the love that has been poured into our hearts by the Helper Himself. Remember this: prayer is not about time; it's about access.

Prayer: *Father, I thank You for sending the Holy Spirit to assist me in every area of my life. I am not alone and will not lean on my own understanding but, in all my ways, acknowledge You as You lead and make straight my path by the leading of the Holy Spirit. Amen.*

DAY 31

"LOVE'S FAITHFULNESS"

Psalms 89:1-5 (MSG) *Your love, God, is my song, and I'll sing it!* ***I'm forever telling everyone how faithful you are.*** *I'll never quit telling the story of your love – How you built the cosmos and guaranteed everything in it. Your love has always been our lives' foundation; your fidelity has been the roof over our world.*

God's faithful love must be the foundation from which we live and through which we perceive and interpret the seasons and circumstances of life. His love is the garrison that surrounds us and keeps the enemy at bay. It's the surplus that continually overflows our cup and the favor that continually places us in positions of advancement. This is the covenanted love that pursues us and is without exhaustion as it looks to express and fulfill its realities in our lives. This is the love that has captured our hearts.

Our text for today in Psalms 89 goes on to say, "Search high and low, scan skies and land, you'll find nothing and no one quite like God. God of the Angel Armies, who is like You, powerful and faithful from every angle?" I like that! No matter the angle you come from, or problem you hold, God is more loyal, constant and steadfast. Radiating both ability and strength. You cannot stand in a place of knowledge where the Father's love is concerned and not be filled with songs of praise and stories of satisfied desires.

Many times, when the Father places vision in our hearts, by either His word or Spirit, there is the temptation to become weary as it is always spoken from beyond the natural boundaries of possibilities, as it is given in the realm of the unseen and through the force of faith. These words spoken must be counted as true for our faithful Creator has declared them. God's vision always carries provision in all things. Every assignment comes with the required action to believe God and to disbelieve the doubts. We must all continue to build our faith in His love and faithfulness as we prepare for the BIG that He has in store for us; for what God speaks He will perform and make good.

Prayer: *Psalms 89:20-24, 33 (MSG) I found (your name here_____) David, my servant, poured holy oil on his head, and I'll keep my hand steadily on him, Yes, I'll stick with him through thick and thin. No enemy will get the best of him, no scoundrel will do him in. I'll weed out all who oppose him, I'll clean out all who hate him. I'm with him for good and **I'll love him forever;** I've set him on high—he's riding high! I'll preserve him eternally in my love, I'll faithfully do all I so solemnly promised. Amen.*

ABOUT THE AUTHOR

In one form or another, Dustin O. Martin has ministered the gospel since childhood. He received his formal education in theology and mission work at Rhema Bible College and Domata School of Missions. In 2012, he and his wife, Mandy, founded Martin Ministries International, through which they spread the message of Jesus Christ around the world on a full-time basis.

Connect with Dustin Martin:

 www.martinministries.tv

 www.facebook.com/dustinomartin

 www.twitter.com/dustinomartin

 www.instagram.com/dustinomartin